W9-AGF-479

BACKYARD EXPLORER

Leaf & Tree Guide

By Rona Beame
Illustrations by Lionel Kalish

Workman Publishing, New York

For three dear friends:
Neila Fisher, Bette Miller, Marjorie Schlenoff

Acknowledgments

For all their help, I would like to thank: Joe Beitel, Jeannie
Fernsworth, Lothian Lynas, and Mike Ruggiero at the New
York Botanical Garden; Ken Finch and Richard Haley at the
New Canaan Nature Center in Connecticut; and the
Chappaqua Library. Thanks, too, to Charles Kreloff for his
design, to Stephen Hughes for seeing it through, and to Frank
Germanotta for the leaf silhouette drawings. And last, but far
from least, thanks to my editor Suzanne Rafer and my copy
editor Mary Wilkinson.

Library of Congress Cataloging-in-Publication Data

Beame, Rona.
    Backyard explorer kit / by Rona Beame ; illustrations by Lionel Kalish.
        p.   cm.
    Includes index.
    Summary: Discusses the types and life cycle of trees and how their leaves function,
explains how to collect and preserve leaves, and suggests leaf and tree projects for the
entire year.
    ISBN 0-89480-343-3 : $9.95
    1. Trees—Juvenile literature.   2. Leaves—Juvenile literature.   3. Leaves—
Collection and preservation—Juvenile literature.   4. Seeds—Collection and
preservation—Juvenile literature.   5. Nature craft—Juvenile literature. [1. Trees.
2. Leaves.   3. Leaves—Collection and preservation.   4. Nature craft.
5. Handicraft.]   I. Kalish, Lionel, ill.   II. Title.
QK475.8.B43   1989
582.16—dc20
                                        88-51582
                                           CIP
                                           AC

Project design: Charles Kreloff with
  Stephen Hughes
Cover and book illustrations: Lionel Kalish
Leaf photographs: Walt Chrynwski

Manufactured in the U.S.A.

Workman Publishing Company, Inc.
708 Broadway
New York, New York 10003

First printing October 1989
10 9 8 7 6 5 4 3 2 1

Contents

Collecting Projects   43

Investigating Trees

Have you ever brought home a bright red autumn leaf and wondered why green leaves turn red in the fall?

Have you ever saved a cone because you liked the way it felt and wondered if there was anything inside?

Have you ever wanted to know what causes those strange bumps you sometimes see on leaves?

Then get set to go on an exciting nature hunt! In the woods and parks, on the city streets—even in your own backyard—you'll track down and identify dozens of leaves, seeds, and cones as you investigate the wonderful world of trees.

You'll become a backyard explorer, and backyard explorers are special people. They are curious. They like to collect things. They like to solve nature's mysteries. They like to have fun.

Whenever backyard explorers go outside, they look around and see what's going on in the trees and on the ground. Have the buds opened yet? Are there flowers or fruit on the twigs? What kind of nuts is that squirrel hoarding for winter?

Winter, spring, summer, or fall, once you're a backyard explorer, there's always something to do outdoors.

The Backyard Explorer Kit

The BACKYARD EXPLORER KIT will help you to understand how trees grow, learn easy tricks to identify the trees around you, and master projects you and your friends will enjoy all year long.

Leaf & Tree Guide:
On each page of
the Collecting
Guide section of this
book is a picture and description of a leaf, seed, nut, cone,
pod, or berry for you to find.
Bring your book along when
you go exploring so you can
easily match up and identify
your discoveries.

Leaf Collecting Envelope: This
giant envelope will protect
the leaves until you get them
home. Place a damp rag or
paper towel in the envelope to
keep leaves from drying out
too fast and curling up.

Leaf Collecting Album: The Leaf Collecting Album
contains 28 sturdy cards for matching, saving, and
displaying the best of your collection.

Press the leaves you find as soon as you get home,
otherwise they'll curl up and be impossible to use. Then
paste or tape each leaf to its matching leaf card. (Pressing and mounting instructions begin on page 43.) If you
wish, put loose-leaf reinforcements around the holes to
strengthen them.

Use the shoelace to string the cards together with
the Leaf Collecting Album cover. The shoelace allows
you to add more pages to the album as your collection
grows.

Turn an empty egg carton, shoebox, or Christmas
card box with a see-through top into a display case for
all the cones and other things you collect. Don't close
the lid for at least several weeks or your discoveries
might get moldy.

What Is a Tree?

More than 20,000 different kinds of trees grow around the world—in the rain forests of the Amazon, in the craters of extinct volcanoes in Africa, on the streets of your neighborhood. But what is it that makes trees unique in the plant kingdom?

Trees differ from all other plants because they are bigger (usually over 12 feet tall) and stronger (with a single main stem, called a trunk, which is made out of wood), and because they live longer (many live for hundreds of years).

When you first look at them, trees don't seem to be doing very much, but each part has a special job to do—from the millions of tiny pores on the leaves to the different layers of the trunk.

The Roots

Unless a tree is upended by a storm, you never get to see its remarkable maze of underground roots. Huge anchoring roots support the tree, reaching deep into the earth and sideways at least as wide as the branches grow, along with a network of medium-size roots. Otherwise, trees would crash down during storms and high winds.

The smaller, delicate feeder roots push out sideways from the bigger roots and are covered with billions of tiny root hairs. These stay close to the surface to feed on the rich topsoil, absorbing the water and minerals the tree must have in order to produce food and grow.

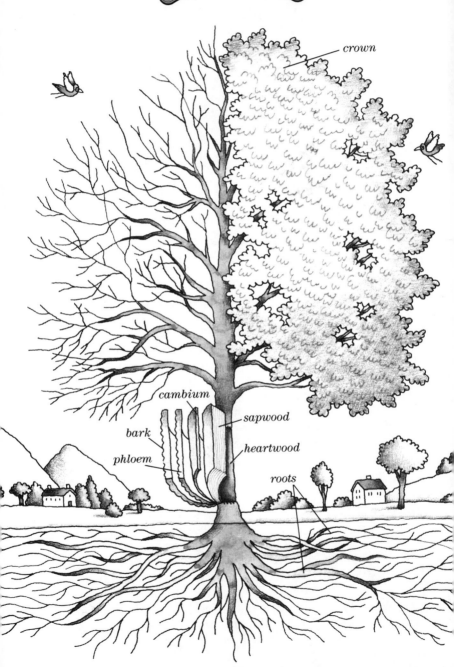

crown

cambium

bark

phloem

sapwood

heartwood

roots

The Trunk

The trunk is made up of separate layers, and each layer has its own job to do.

The tough outer layer is the bark. Its job is to protect the tree. The bark keeps the tree cool in summer and warm in winter, stops the tree from losing too much water, and guards it from insects, fire, and disease.

The spongy inner bark, or phloem, is a highway for food. Sugar sap, made by the leaves, travels down the inner bark to feed the twigs, branches, trunk, and roots. Eventually, old inner bark becomes outer bark.

Although the green cambium layer is thinner than a piece of paper, it is the most important part of the tree because it is in charge of making new inner bark and new sapwood. This is how the trunk grows wider.

The sapwood, or xylem, is the tree's second highway. This is the road for water and minerals (called root sap) to travel up from the roots to the leaves. The sapwood is also a storehouse for extra food.

The heartwood, at the center of the tree, is what makes the tree strong and rigid.

The Crown

The crown of a tree includes many of the things that make a tree look beautiful—the branches, twigs, leaves, flowers, and fruit. The crown has two main jobs—to make food for the tree and to make seeds. The leaves make food. The flowers and fruit make and protect the seeds, which will become new trees.

Two Kinds of Trees

Trees are divided into two major categories. *Deciduous* (dah-'sid-joo-us) trees, such as maples and birches, lose their leaves in autumn, remain leafless through the winter, and grow new leaves in spring. Most, but not all, have broad, flat leaves and are called *broadleaf* trees.

Evergreen trees, such as pines and spruces, keep their leaves all year long, even during winter. Most, but not all, have narrow, flattened or needle-like leaves. Trees that carry their seeds in cones are called *conifers*. Most evergreens belong to this group.

NONCONFORMISTS

Even in nature, there are exceptions to the rule. Here are two: *Deciduous conifers* (such as larches) lose their needles in autumn. *Broadleaf evergreens* (such as hollies) keep their wide, flat leaves year round.

evergreen tree   *broadleaf tree*

Leaves

When people think about trees, the first thing they think of are the leaves. Leaves are a food factory. They make the tree's food (sugar sap) out of root sap (water and minerals), carbon dioxide (from the air), and sunshine with the help of a green chemical called chlorophyll (chlorophyll is what makes leaves green). This food-manufacturing process is called photosynthesis.

Why Broadleaf Trees Have Big Leaves

Most broadleaf trees have big leaves because they have to make enough food in six months to last the tree all year long. The bigger the leaf, the more sunshine it can absorb, and the more food it can make.

When a deciduous broadleaf tree loses its leaves in autumn, it lives on the food stored in the trunk and branches. During winter, the tree slows down a lot and doesn't use much food. But when spring comes, a tree needs lots of food for its new buds.

What Each Part of a Broad Leaf Does

Stem: The leaf stem attaches the leaf to its twig. Stand underneath a leafy tree and look up. See how leaves are arranged on a branch so that each one gets some sun. This is because sunlight is so important for making food that if one leaf blocks all the light from another, the shaded leaf will turn yellow and die. Notice that the leaf stems are of different lengths—shorter or longer stems find their leaf a place in the sun.

The leaf stem is the pipeline through which root sap and sugar sap travel in and out of the leaf. And it is flexible so that during a storm the leaf can flap back and forth like a kite on a string. That way the wind won't rip it off.

Veins: The lacy veins are the leaf's skeleton. They stiffen the leaf so its surface is exposed to light and air.

Veins look delicate, but they are the mini-tubes through which root sap and sugar sap pass throughout the leaf.

Surface: The outer skin of a leaf is water-proof. Many leaves also have a waxy coating. The wax stops the leaf from losing too much water and also helps protect the leaf from insects.

Pores: Every leaf has millions of tiny pores, or stomata, which let the tree "breathe." Most are on the bottom side of

the leaf. Leaves take in air through these pores, using the carbon dioxide for photosynthesis; then they release oxygen and water vapor into the atmosphere, and draw up more water from the roots. You can't see it, but a tree is breathing out water vapor all day long.

Hairs: There are also tiny hairs on the underside of many leaves—you can actually feel fuzz on some leaves. The hairs protect the leaf from insects and drying winds, and also keep rainwater from coating the surface, which would prevent the pores from breathing.

Drip tips: Pointy leaf tips and lobes help rainwater run off a leaf more quickly.

The Palm Tree

A palm tree combines qualities of both broadleaf and evergreen trees, and so it is known as a broadleaf evergreen. It usually doesn't have any branches. Instead, the enormous leaves grow only at the top of the trunk, and they are shaped like fans or feathers.

If you live in the north, you won't see any palm trees outside. They grow only in warm climates.

Evergreen Leaves:
The Tough Guys

Winter cold doesn't kill narrow-leaved evergreen leaves because they are much tougher than the delicate leaves that grow on deciduous broadleaf trees.

Skinny evergreen needles won't rip in the wind, and snow will slide off them. Also, a thick layer of wax coats each needle, preventing it from losing too much of the precious water inside and drying out.

Each evergreen needle has only one or two veins, which run down the center of the leaf and transport root sap and sugar sap into and out of the leaf.

Evergreen needles can't make as much food as the large broad leaves do, but they don't have to. Because all of the needles don't fall off in autumn, they continue to make food throughout the year—except for freezing days when everything works in slow motion.

Evergreen trees can grow in places where broadleaf trees have a hard time surviving—from the freezing Arctic, to wind-swept mountains, to furnace-hot deserts.

The Ginkgo Tree

Ginkgo trees have cones, like most evergreens, and broad leaves, like most deciduous trees, but they don't belong to either group. They are the only survivors of a family of trees that were alive almost 200 million years ago—when dinosaurs were stomping through ancient forests!

The Life Cycle of a Broadleaf Tree

 ## Winter: Look for Buds

In winter the tree lies dormant. Its growth slows down, its food manufacturing activities grind almost to a halt, its roots stop drawing much water from the earth, its branches are bare and seemingly lifeless. But deep within the buds, the leaves—and on some, the flowers— are already growing, protected by hard, overlapping scales. The buds begin to swell.

Spring: Flowers and Leaves Bloom

As spring nears, the air warms, the ground thaws, the tree reawakens. Sap rises through its trunk; the fallen seeds take root, and their stems reach for light. The buds burst open to reveal tiny, delicate flowers and leaves. Some have petals; others have drooping tails called catkins. Flowers that are fertilized swell to become fruits, bearing the seeds inside.

 ## Summer: Look for Fruits

In summer, as the seeds develop and the fruits continue to mature, the flowers dry up and fall off. The tree grows, its leaves hard at work manufacturing food. Tiny buds appear—these will lie dormant until next spring

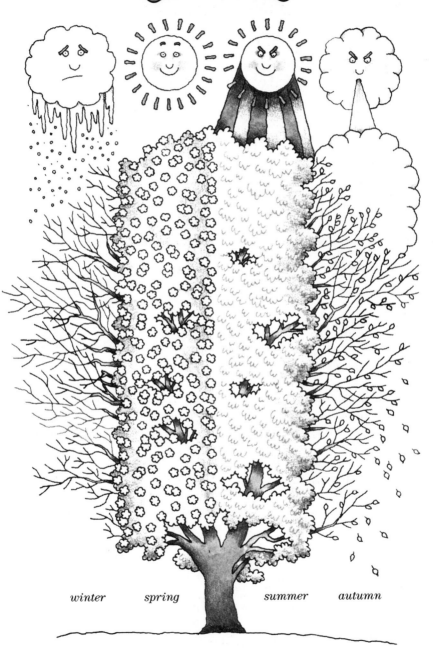

winter   *spring*   *summer*   *autumn*

approaches. As summer ends fruits of all kinds ripen: berries, nuts, pods, capsules. Within each of them are seeds, and each seed contains all the parts it needs to make an entire new tree.

Autumn: Collect Fruits and Seeds

As autumn comes, the ripe fruits with the ripe seeds fall to the ground. The leaves turn color and they also fall. The life of the tree once again slows—until springtime and the beginning of a new cycle.

Why Leaves Turn Color

Broadleaf trees get rid of their leaves in autumn so they won't die of thirst in the winter. Leaves use up great quantities of water, so without leaves a tree doesn't need nearly as much. When water in the ground freezes, the roots can no longer suck it up, but the leafless tree can live on water it has stored.

As summer ends, the days get shorter and the weather gets cold. Broadleaf trees know that now it is time for them to shed their leaves.

The green chlorophyll in the leaves is broken down and removed. All along there were other colors in the leaves, but there was so much chlorophyll you couldn't see them. Now they have their chance. Leaves turn red, orange, yellow, purple, and brown.

A corky layer forms where the stem of each leaf is attached to the twig. Now nothing can get into or out of the leaves, and soon they break off and fall to the ground.

How Seeds Travel

To grow into new trees, seedlings must have plenty of sunlight, water, and minerals. If they stayed under the parent tree, they would be too crowded; also the parent tree's crown would shade them from the sun, and its enormous roots would use up most of the water and minerals in the soil. So to survive, the ripe seeds must travel from the parent tree.

Some seeds are carried away by animals either in the fruits or nuts they eat or bury (and sometimes forget about) or on their fur. Some seeds travel by wind or water to new rooting ground, and some seeds are scattered when the fruits carrying them pop open and shoot them out.

BACKYARD EXPLORER

The Collecting Guide

O n each col-
lecting page
you'll find a
picture of a leaf, fruit,
or seed, clues to help you find it, and
a list of some trees it grows on.

Although some trees grow all across the country,
others naturally grow only in certain areas. But people
love to plant trees from other parts of the world in their
own parks, city streets, or backyards, so don't be surprised if you find a tree that "doesn't belong" growing
in your neighborhood.

The map on page 23 shows the United States divided into five areas: Northwest, Southwest, Central,
Northeast, and Southeast. Canada has been divided into
three areas: Western Canada (including Alaska), Central
Canada, and Eastern Canada. On pages 24 and 25 is a list
of the trees mentioned in this book and where they grow.

The Shapes of Leaves

Trees come in all shapes and sizes, and each
type of tree has its own distinctive type of
leaf. So at first, being able to name a specific
leaf seems like a very difficult task.

But the shape of almost every leaf fits
into one of just nine easy categories. All you
have to do is look carefully at a leaf's shape
and figure out which one of those categories

The Explorer's Code

- Trees are living things that must be treated well in order to survive.
- Never peel bark from a tree or you'll harm it. Trees need their bark just like people need their skin.
- You will not hurt a tree if you take just several leaves or a twig from it, but do it very carefully.
- Never break off a piece of branch or a twig from a tree. Instead, with an adult's help, cut small sections with pruning shears.
- Never pick anything when you are exploring a nature preserve. If you want a sample from a neighbor's tree, be sure to ask permission.
- Never eat anything that grows on a tree—or on any other plant—unless you've checked it out with your parents. Some fruits, berries, leaves, flowers, seeds, and other parts of plants are poisonous.

it belongs to. Then you've taken the first important step to unlocking the key to its identity.

"Simple" leaves on broadleaf trees are made up of one solid piece. Their outlines fall into four basic shapes: smooth; toothed; hand-shaped; and feather-shaped.

"Compound" leaves on broadleaf trees are made up of more than one leaflet attached to the same leaf stem. They come in two basic patterns: hand-shaped; and feather-shaped.

To tell a leaf from a leaflet, look for where the "leaf" joins the twig. A bud will grow only where the main stem of a whole leaf meets the twig. So if you see a bud, you've found a complete leaf. If you don't see a bud, it's a leaflet from a compound leaf.

simple leaf ← *bud* *compound leaf* *bud* → *leaflets*

Most evergreen leaves are grouped into three basic shapes: cluster needles; single needles; and scaly leaves that look like needles.

When to Collect Leaves

You don't have to wait until autumn to collect leaves. Many trees have branches low enough for you to reach. And you can usually find plenty of leaves on the ground that have been blown down by spring and summer winds.

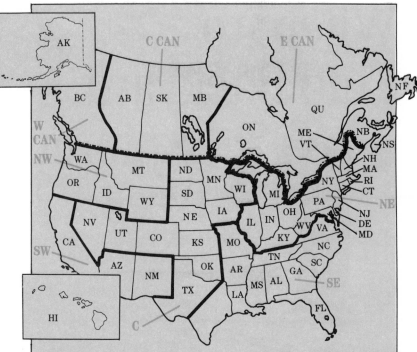

U.S. and Canada Map Code

NW: Northwest states

SW: Southwest states

W: Northwest and Southwest states

C: Central states

NE: Northeast states

SE: Southeast states

E: Northeast and Southeast states

W Can: Western Canadian provinces plus Alaska

C Can: Central Canadian provinces

E Can: Eastern Canadian provinces

Where to Find Backyard Explorer Trees

African tuliptree   Hawaii
American beech   E; E Can
American bladdernut   C, E
American chestnut   E
American elm   C, E; E Can
American sycamore   C, E;
  E Can
Arizona walnut   SW, C
Atlantic white cedar   E
Austrian pine   NW, C, NE

Baldcypress   C, E
Balsam fir   C, NE; C Can, E Can
Bigleaf maple   W; W Can
Bigtooth aspen   C, NE
Bitternut hickory   C, E; E Can
Black cottonwood   W, C
Blackgum (pepperidge)   C, E
Black locust   C, E
Black oak   C, E; E Can

Black walnut   C, E
Bur oak   C, E; C Can, E Can

Cabbage palmetto   SE
California black oak   W
California buckeye   SW
California juniper   SW
California sycamore   SW
California walnut   SW
California Washingtonia   SW
Canyon live oak   W
Chestnut oak   C, E
Coast (California) live oak   SW
Coconut palm   Hawaii, SE
Colorado spruce   SW, C
Common hoptree   SW, C, E
Common juniper   All Areas

Douglas fir   W; W Can

Eastern cottonwood   C, E
Eastern hemlock   NE; E Can
Eastern redbud   C, E
Eastern red cedar   C, E; E Can
Eastern white pine   C, E;
  C Can, E Can
European larch   All Areas
European linden   NW, C, E

Flowering dogwood   C, E; E Can

Gambel oak   SW, C
Ginkgo   All Areas

Honey locust   C, E
Horsechestnut   All Areas

Incense cedar   W
Italian cypress   SW, SE
Interior live oak   W

Jack pine   C, E; C Can, E Can
Japanese pagodatree (Chinese
   scholartree)   All Areas
Jeffrey pine   W

Kentucky coffeetree   C, E
Kukui (candlenut tree)   Hawaii

Live oak   SE
Loblolly pine   SE
Lodgepole pine   W, C; W Can
Lombardy poplar   All Areas
London planetree   All Areas
Longleaf pine   SE

Mexican Washingtonia   SW
Mimosa (silktree)   C, E

Northern catalpa   C, E
Northern red oak
   C, E; E Can
Northern white cedar
   C, E; C Can, E Can
Norway maple   All
   Areas
Norway spruce   NW,
   C, E

Ohio buckeye   C, E
Oregon white oak   NW;
   W Can
Osage orange   C

Pacific dogwood   W;
   W Can
Paper birch   NW, C, NE;
   All Can

Pecan   C, SE
Peachleaf willow   C, NE; C Can
Pin oak   C, E
Pitch pine   E; E Can
Post oak   C, E

Quaking aspen   W, C, NE;
   All Can

Red maple   C, E; E Can, C Can
Rocky Mountain juniper   W, C;
   W Can
Royal palm   SE
Russian olive   NW, C, NE

Sarawa false cypress   All Areas
Scarlet oak   C, E
Scots (Scotch) pine   NW, C, NE
Shagbark hickory   C, E; E Can
Siberian elm   W, C, SE
Silver maple   C, E
Sitka spruce   NW; W Can
Southern catalpa   E
Southern magnolia   SE
Sugar maple   C, E
Sugar pine   W
Sweetgum   C, E

Tamarack   C, NE; All Can
Tamarisk   SW, C
Texas buckeye   C
Tree of heaven (ailanthus)
   All Areas
Tuliptree (yellow poplar)   E

Virginia pine   E

Weeping willow   All Areas
Western hemlock   NW; W Can
Western larch   NW, C; W Can
Western red cedar   NW; W Can
Western white pine   W; W Can
White ash   C, E; E Can
White oak   C, E
White poplar   All Areas
White spruce   C, NE; All Can
Willow oak   C, E

FIND

Smooth-edged Simple Leaf

Look for: A leaf that has a very smooth edge. Run your finger around it. You shouldn't feel any bumps or teeth.

Many smooth-edged simple leaves are oval:
- African tuliptree
- Flowering dogwood (shown)
- Osage orange
- Pacific dogwood
- Southern magnolia (evergreen)

Some are heart-shaped:
- Eastern redbud
- Northern catalpa
- Southern catalpa (shown)

Others are very skinny:
- Interior live oak
- Live oak
- Russian olive
- Willow oak (shown)

For Super Explorers: Note that the flowering dogwood leaf, above, is fattest in the middle. Collect some oval leaves with their stems. See where they are fattest—at the top, bottom, or middle. If you're not sure, bend the leaf in half to find out.

FIND

Toothed Simple Leaf

Look for: A leaf that has toothed or jagged edges similar to the teeth on a saw. Toothed leaves can be oval, heart-shaped, or skinny; they are the most common leaves.

Many leaves have big sharp teeth:
- American beech
- American elm (shown)
- Coast (California) live oak
- European linden

Others have tiny teeth:
- Lombardy poplar
- Paper birch (shown)
- Quaking aspen
- Siberian elm
- Weeping willow

Other leaves have rounded teeth:
- Bigtooth aspen
- Black cottonwood
- Eastern cottonwood (shown)

For Super Explorers: Look for leaves that have groups of little teeth between each of the big teeth.

FIND

Hand-shaped Simple Leaf

Look for: A leaf that is shaped like your hand with its fingers spread. In a hand-shaped leaf, the main veins begin at the stem and run out at angles into the lobes. Hand-shaped leaves can have anywhere from three to seven fingers, or lobes.

Some are deeply lobed:
- Bigleaf maple
- California sycamore
- Silver maple
- Sugar maple
- Sweetgum (shown)

Other leaves have shallow lobes:
- American sycamore
- Kukui (candlenut tree)
- Norway maple (shown)
- Tuliptree (yellow poplar)

For Super Explorers: Like human fingerprints, no two leaves are exactly the same. It is easy to spot the differences in hand-shaped leaves. Take some leaves from the same tree, lay them on top of one another, and compare.

FIND

Hand-shaped Compound Leaf

Look for: A leaf that looks like the hand-shaped simple leaf, but whose lobes or fingers are cut into separate leaflets. They all radiate from one point, like the points on a star.

Sometimes it's hard to tell a leaf from a leaflet. Look at where the leaf joins the twig. Remember that a bud will grow only where the main stem of the whole leaf meets the twig. So if you see a bud—it's a leaf. If not— it's a leaflet.

Hand-shaped compound leaves can have anywhere from three to eleven leaflets.

 Three leaflets:
- American bladder-nut
- Common hoptree (shown)

 Five to seven leaflets:
- California buckeye
- Horsechestnut
- Ohio buckeye (shown)

 Seven to eleven leaflets:
- Texas buckeye (shown)

FIND

Feather-shaped Simple Leaf

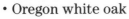

Look for: A leaf that reminds you of
a feather. It has a long main vein that goes
from the stem to the tip. On each side of this vein,
opposite each other, are the feathery lobes.

Feather-shaped leaves grow on oak trees. There are
two main groups of oak trees: black oaks and white oaks.

White oak leaves have rounded lobes:
- Bur oak
- Gambel oak
- Oregon white oak
- Post oak
- White oak (shown)

Black oaks have leaves with pointy lobes:
- Black oak (shown)
- California black oak
- Northern red oak
- Pin oak
- Scarlet oak

For Super Explorers: Some oak leaves, like the chestnut oak of the East or the canyon live oak of the West,
don't have lobes. See how many different-shaped oak
leaves you can find.

All oak trees have acorns. When you're searching
for oak leaves, look for acorns under a tree.

FIND

Feather-shaped Compound Leaf

Look for: A leaf that looks like a feather and is divided into leaflets growing opposite each other along a central stem. Remember to find the bud on the twig—then you will know if you are looking at a leaf or a leaflet.

Some feather-shaped compound leaves have hundreds of small leaflets. If the leaflets grow on each side of the main stem, they are called pinnate. If the main stem has little stems on each side, and the leaflets are attached to those little stems, the leaves are called bipinnate.

Some feather-shaped compound leaves are pinnate:
- Bitternut hickory
- Black locust
- Black walnut
- California walnut
- Tree of heaven (ailanthus; shown)
- White ash

Some are bipinnate:
- Kentucky coffeetree
- Mimosa (silktree; shown)

FIND

Alternate and Opposite Leaves

Look for: The way broad leaves are arranged on the twig. On some broadleaf trees, the leaves grow opposite each other on the twig. On others they grow in alternate places along the twig.

Most trees have alternate leaves:
- American beech
- Bur oak
- Blackgum (pepperidge)
- Canyon live oak
- Southern magnolia
- Weeping willow
- White oak (shown)

But many trees have opposite leaves:
- Flowering dogwood
- Horsechestnut
- Ohio buckeye
- Red maple (shown)
- Rocky Mountain maple
- White ash

 FIND

Palm Leaf

Look for: Huge leaves shaped like feathers or fans.

 Palm leaves can be either feather-shaped compound leaves:
- Coconut palm (shown)
- Royal palm

 Or fan-shaped simple leaves (that often look almost like compound leaves with separate leaflets):
- Cabbage palmetto (shown)
- California Washingtonia
- Mexican Washingtonia

Note: This hunt is only for explorers who live in warm climates or who are lucky enough to vacation there.

FIND

Ginkgo Leaf

Look for: A leaf that looks like a duck's foot or fan. The edges of the ginkgo leaf are wavy and many have a small V-shaped wedge cut out. Notice how long the stem is.
   Look for the ginkgo tree on city streets.

Cluster Needles

Look for: An evergreen tree with long needles that grow in bunches, or clusters. Each cluster grows from one place on the twig of a pine tree.

Some pine needles grow in clusters of two:
- Austrian pine (shown)
- Jack pine
- Lodgepole pine
- Scots (Scotch) pine
- Virginia pine

Some grow in clusters of three:
- Jeffrey pine
- Loblolly pine (shown)
- Longleaf pine
- Pitch pine

Other needles grow in clusters of five:
- Eastern white pine (shown)
- Sugar pine
- Western white pine

Some pines have more than ten needles per cluster:
- European larch (deciduous; shown)
- Tamarack (deciduous)
- Western larch (deciduous)

FIND

Single Needles

Look for: An evergreen tree that has short, stiff needles. Each needle grows from its own place on the twig, like the teeth on a comb. Most are no more than an inch long.

Some single needles grow opposite each other on the twig:
- Baldcypress (deciduous)
- Balsam fir
- Douglas fir
- Eastern hemlock (shown)
- Western hemlock

Others grow all around the twig:
- Colorado spruce
- Norway spruce (shown)
- Sitka spruce
- White spruce

For Super Explorers: You will need sharp eyes to find a single needle with four sides and a sharp, pointy tip. Also see if you can find a needle with a rounded tip.

FIND

Scaly Leaves

Look for: An evergreen tree with leaves that resemble needles but actually are tiny, overlapping scales like the petals on a rosebud. You have to look very closely to see the scales because they are only ⅛ inch long or smaller.

You can't see the twigs underneath scaly leaves because the scales are so close together that they hide the twigs.

Some scaly leaves have flat branches; they look like lacy ferns:
- Incense cedar
- Northern white cedar (shown)
- Sarawa false cypress
- Western red cedar

Other scaly leaves are smaller so the twigs look almost bare; they branch in all directions and are often prickly:
- California juniper
- Eastern red cedar (shown)
- Italian cypress

Note: Wear gloves or use a piece of paper towel when you pick twigs with sharp needles.

FIND

Leaves Attacked by Insects

Note: Search for these leaves in the late summer and autumn.

 Look for: The Swiss-cheese leaf. Caterpillars and leaf beetles have made a good dinner of these leaves. Sometimes, it seems like there are more holes than leaf.

 Look for: The skeleton leaf. This leaf is so eaten away by insects that there is practically nothing left—just veins and a stem.

 Look for: The gall leaf. This leaf has strange bumps, of varying shapes, sizes, and colors, which may be hairy, sticky, or smooth. The bumps are galls, or insect homes, made by gall wasps and gall flies.

Oak leaves are some of the best places for finding galls. You might even find several different kinds on one leaf. Put the flattest galls on your leaf album card and save the rest for a gall project (page 56).

Look for: A leaf miner's leaf. Leaf miners are tiny insects that live between the top and bottom layers of leaves. They begin their lives as eggs laid on the outside of a leaf. When they hatch, each leaf miner burrows its way inside the leaf and spends its youth alone, tunneling through the leaf tissue and eating as it goes.

Look carefully and you'll observe that the leaf miner's tunnel is very narrow at one end and wider at the other. That's because the insect gets fatter as it eats and tunnels along!

See if you can find a tiny exit hole at the wider end of the tunnel—most leaf miners leave the tunnel when they become adults.

Look for Beautiful Autumn Leaves

This hunt is only for explorers who live in cold climates where the trees turn color in autumn. Look for red, purple, orange, and yellow leaves, and some that even have more than one color. Try to find as many beautiful and unusual multi-colored leaves as possible.

Notice that autumn leaves are tougher and stiffer than the delicate, soft leaves of spring. That's because spring leaves are filled with water and autumn leaves are dry.

FIND

Surprise Packages

Hunting for Dry Fruits, Seeds, and Berries

T rees produce lots of things you can collect and study besides leaves. Track down all the cones, pods, nuts, balls, berries, and seeds pictured on the following pages—and remember to collect extras for the projects.

Pods: Pods look like stringbeans or pea pods hanging from branches. They get hard and leathery when they ripen, then split open to release their bean-shaped seeds.

- Black locust (2-4″ long; shown, top)
- Honey locust (6-16″ long; shown, bottom)
- Japanese pagoda-tree (Chinese scholartree; 2-3″ long)

Winged "seeds": Many seeds are housed in fruits that look like papery wings. Often they grow on the biggest trees, high up where they can catch the strongest breezes. When the seeds within the fruits are

ripe, they fall off the tree. Their wings spin round and round, slowing the fall so they can stay up in the air longer, and giving the wind a chance to carry them farther away from the parent tree. Look for winged seeds in the spring and fall.

- Common hoptree (round wing)
- Norway maple (double wing; shown, top)
- Norway Spruce (single wing; shown, bottom)
- Tree of heaven (ailanthus; oblong wing)
- White ash (single wing)

Hairy seeds: Hairy seeds, which grow inside fruits called capsules, are even lighter than winged seeds. When they escape from their fruits, these seeds are attached to fine white, cottony hairs that help them sail through the air. Riding the winds, they can travel for miles. On some summer days, the air is filled with them—it seems like it is snowing!

- Peachleaf willow (shown)
- Tamarisk
- Weeping willow
- White poplar

Small brown balls: In the autumn when the leaves are gone, you can clearly see brown balls, about an inch in diameter, dangling from the branches by their long stems.

- American sycamore (slightly bumpy)
- London planetree (bristly)
- Sweetgum (prickly; shown)

Acorns: Acorns grow on oak trees all over the world. There are at least 50 different kinds of oaks in North America.

Their acorns come in many different shapes—but they always have a scaly cup at the base.

- Bur oak (big cup)
- Coast (California) live oak (long and skinny)

- Northern red oak (shallow cup; shown)
- Pin oak (short and fat)

Spiny-husked nuts: Spiny-husked nuts have either sharp thorns like a porcupine or spikes like the bottom of a golf shoe.

- American chestnut (prickly; shown)
- Horsechestnut (spiky; poisonous seeds)

- Ohio buckeye (spiky; poisonous seeds)

Fleshy and Dry Fruits

A tree's fruit is the part that holds and protects the seeds. Everyone knows that apples and oranges are fruits. These are known as fleshy fruits. But pods, nut husks, brown balls, and winged seeds (called keys) are also fruits because they contain the tree's seeds. These are called dry fruits.

On some fruits (such as peaches or plums) the part you eat surrounds the seed or seeds. But on other fruits (like walnuts or coconuts), it is the inner seed itself, the part we call the nutmeat, that is good to eat.

Smooth-husked nuts: With their husks on, smooth-husked nuts look nothing like the nuts we buy in the store. Instead, they resemble little lemons dangling from trees. Only when you take their husks off do you find the shell, like the wrinkled walnut or smooth pecan, that we commonly see.

Note: Walnut husks can dye hands brownish black.

- Arizona walnut
- Bitternut hickory
- Shagbark hickory (shown)

Cones: Cones grow on most evergreen trees. At first they are soft and green, but after their seeds ripen they turn brown and become woody. It may take several years for the seeds inside to ripen.

There are two winged seeds on each scale of most cones. When its seeds are ripe, the cone opens its scales so the seeds can fly away. Unlike the fruit of broadleaf trees, some cones stay on the trees long after their seeds have gone. Most of the open cones you find on the ground do not have seeds inside.

- Atlantic white cedar (¼″ long)
- Eastern white pine (4-8″ long; shown)
- Sugar pine (11-18″ long)
- Western hemlock (¾-1″ long)

Blue "berries": The blue "berries" found on many juniper and red cedar trees are really tiny blue cones. If you look very closely, you will see the overlapping scales.

- Common juniper
- Eastern red cedar (shown)
- Rocky Mountain juniper

Collecting Projects

There are lots of interesting things to do with every part of a tree—any time of the year. Leaves, dried fruits, nuts, flowers, and seeds can be used to create artistic paintings and collages or transformed into one-of-a-kind, hand-crafted gifts.

Investigations into how trees change through the year and what happens to fallen leaves—along with experiments like capturing water from leaves, growing your own buds, and hatching galls—will help you better understand the mysteries of a tree. And the more you learn, the more fun you'll have observing the trees around you.

How to Press Leaves

Before you can mount leaves in your album or do many of the backyard explorer projects, you'll need to press the leaves you've collected. Do this as soon as you get home or they'll curl up and be unusable.

Here are two easy meth-
ods for pressing leaves:
one takes two weeks
and one is super quick.

Two-week Method

Pat wet leaves dry, and cut
off any thick stems. Lay them flat between four sheets
of newspaper, making sure they don't touch each other.

Weight down your leaves by placing something very
heavy on top—fat telephone books are excellent. After
about two weeks, carefully remove the leaves from the
newspaper. They are now ready to mount in your album.

Store extra pressed leaves in a box so they won't
get hurt.

Quick Method

Not everyone has the patience to wait two weeks for
leaves to dry. Here is a quick way to press leaves, using
an iron. You'll need the assistance of an adult.

Have an adult set up an ironing board and preheat
a dry iron on the permanent press setting for two
minutes.

Careful!

Stand the iron on its end when not in use. Always
turn off and unplug an iron as soon as you are
finished using it.

Place a thin piece of cardboard on the ironing board, and cover it with a sheet of wax paper a little larger than your leaf. Place your leaf on top, cover it with another sheet of wax paper, and then a cotton rag (part of an old sheet would be perfect).

Iron back and forth all over, making sure that each part of the leaf gets ironed for at least the count of 20.

Remove the rag and cardboard. Carefully peel the wax paper from the leaf. Feel the leaf. It should be perfectly flat and have a slightly waxy surface, which will make it stronger. Now it is ready for mounting.

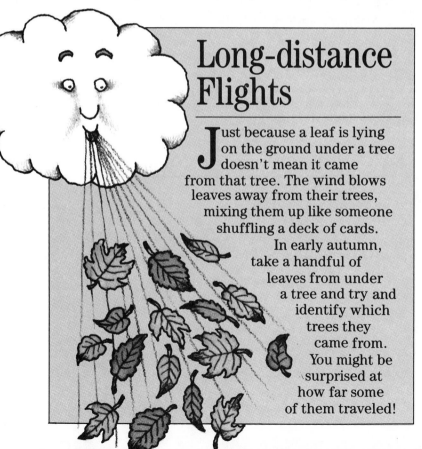

Long-distance Flights

Just because a leaf is lying on the ground under a tree doesn't mean it came from that tree. The wind blows leaves away from their trees, mixing them up like someone shuffling a deck of cards.

In early autumn, take a handful of leaves from under a tree and try and identify which trees they came from. You might be surprised at how far some of them traveled!

BACKYARD EXPLORER

Mounting Leaves

After your leaves are pressed, you are ready to mount them on their album cards. Match the shape of your leaf to the correct album card. If you haven't already done so, make sure to cut off any thick stems. Paste or tape your leaf to its card.

Making Leaves Shiny and Bright

When you apply découpage glue to a leaf, it strengthens the leaf and makes it look shiny. You can buy the glue in an art supply store and use it to "paint" the mounted leaves on your album cards. Découpage glue is easy to use. You can clean your brush and any spills with water.

Cover your work surface with newspaper. Dip your brush into the jar of découpage glue and spread it evenly over the mounted leaf.

Let your cards dry overnight.

Grow Buds

When you look up at the buds in late winter and early spring, do you wonder what's inside? Here's a chance to find out before everyone else does. You'll need an adult to help you collect some twigs.

YOU'LL NEED:

Garden shears (use only with an adult's help)
Twigs with buds on them
Jar with water

1 In February, when buds are still tightly closed, have an adult help you cut off a 12-inch twig from several different kinds of trees. Use garden shears for a sharp, clean cut, and make the cuts at an angle. Never take more than you need. Make sure you take a twig from your favorite tree (see page 48).

2 Fill a jar with water, and put in the twigs. Place it on a sunny windowsill in a warm room. Change the water every few days.

3 Check your twigs daily, and notice how the buds begin to swell. Finally, the flower buds will burst open. Leaf buds will take a little more time.

Find a Favorite Tree

One pretty day in spring, take a walk and pick out your favorite broadleaf tree. Maybe you like the way its bark feels, or think the flowers are beautiful. Or maybe it grows outside your bedroom window, and you have known this tree for a long time.

Select a tree that is nearby, that is easy to remember, and that has some low branches you can reach.

Throughout the year observe what happens to your tree. In the spring does it develop leaves or flowers first? What kind of leaves does it have? What colors do they turn in autumn? Take pictures of your favorite tree in every season.

Find the album pages that say "Favorite Tree" on top. Put leaves and photographs of your tree on them. Mount extra photos on oaktag or colored paper. Write the date on which each picture was taken and what was happening to the tree at the time of the photograph.

If your tree belongs to a neighbor, ask permission before you pick things from it.

A Secret Way to Identify Your Tree: You can mark your favorite tree so it will always be recognizable. But if your tree is in a park or on a city street, you can't tie a name tag or ribbon around it. You have to find a secret way to identify it.

Find a big, unusual-looking stone and write your name on it with a black waterproof marking pen; then put the stone under your tree with the writing side face down. No one will ever know that this is your secret tree.

The Dead Leaf Mystery

Why aren't we up to our necks in old leaves? What's happened to the billions of dead leaves that fell last autumn? They all were not raked up neatly. But somehow, they disappeared without our noticing. Bacteria, insects, and tiny animals turned the dead leaves back into soil and food for trees and plants. Would you like to see some of the members of this huge cleanup army?

YOU'LL NEED:

Long-handled spoon or small shovel
Large plastic container or plastic garbage bag
Newspaper
Small clean jar
Magnifying glass (optional)

1 Find a tree that still has some rotting leaves and twigs from last year beneath it. Scoop up some of the damp, loose soil underneath.

2 Lay some newspaper on the ground outside and spread a very thin (¼-inch-deep) layer of soil on top.

3 Use the spoon or shovel to inspect the soil. Examine the pieces of rotting leaves, twigs, and nuts. You should find both plant eaters and meat eaters (they eat the plant eaters) in the soil. Most of the meat eaters seem to rush around; the plant eaters move more slowly. Some spiders and centipedes are poisonous, so be very careful not to touch them.

4 See if you can find these plant eaters in the soil: snails, slugs, ants, grubs, springtails, millipedes.

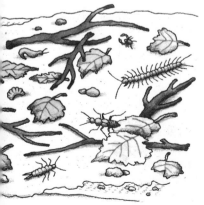

5 Look for these meat eaters: spiders, false scorpions, centipedes, rove beetles. Mites eat both plants and animals.

6 See how many different kinds of insects and tiny animals you can find. Put each one in a small, clean jar (like a baby food jar) while you study it. When you're finished, let them go—they have a job to do.

Leafcards and Bookmarks

You can use leaves to make wonderful leaf postcards to send your friends or bookmarks to give as gifts.

YOU'LL NEED:

Pencil
Ruler
Unlined index cards
Postage stamps
Scissors

Clear contact paper
Piece of cardboard
Cellophane tape
Pressed leaves

Leafcards

1 Draw a line down the middle of an index card. On the left side, write a message to a friend; on the right, put a postage stamp and your friend's name and address.

2 Cut a piece of clear contact paper slightly larger than the index card. Peel off the backing and lay the contact paper on the cardboard, sticky side up, with tape holding down each corner.

3 Choose pressed leaves that will look pretty on the index card—either one big leaf or several small leaves or evergreen needles. Place the leaves on the sticky surface of the contact paper. Press them down, and cover them with the blank side of the index card.

4 Remove the tape, turn the card over, and press your fingers around the edges of the leaves to make them stand out more clearly.

5 Trim off the extra contact paper. Your leaf postcard is ready to mail.

Bookmarks

1 To make a bookmark, draw a line down the middle of the long side of an index card, and cut it.

2 Using skinny broad leaves or evergreen needles, follow Steps 2 to 5 (above). Leaf bookmarks make fun gifts that are also useful!

Capturing Water

Every day, the roots of a tree send up enormous amounts of water to the leaves. The leaves breathe it out through tiny holes, or pores, most of which are on the underside of the leaf.

You cannot see the water leaving because it is invisible—it has been turned into water vapor, which is a gas. But you can capture the vapor as it leaves the leaf and turn it back into water.

YOU'LL NEED:

Small pebble
Small plastic sandwich bag
Twist tie
Measuring spoon

1 On a hot summer day, put a small pebble in a plastic sandwich bag. Put the plastic bag over a leaf that gets a lot of sunshine, and tie it tightly to the stem with the twist tie.

2 Come back in a few hours. Already you will be able to see beads of moisture inside the plastic bag. The vapor is turning back into water.

3 Check each day to observe how much water is gathering in your bag. At the end of a week, carefully take off the bag. Use a measuring spoon to find out how much water is in the bag.

A small leaf that gets a lot of sunshine will give off about ½ teaspoon of water in a week. Find out how much a big leaf will give off.

There are over 100,000 leaves on an average tree. Just think about how much water trees send up into the air each day, especially in summer!

Giant Air Conditioners

One big tree can have the cooling power of many air conditioners. A tree's crown makes shade, and its leaves give off moisture, which cools the air.

Hatching Leaf Galls

Leaf galls are insect homes that are found on leaves. It is possible to actually "hatch" a leaf gall.

1 In autumn when the leaves are beginning to fall, look for bumpy galls on oak and willow leaves. There are hundreds of different kinds of galls, so you may find many different types—even on the same leaf. Galls can be as small as a pin head or as big as a button.

2 Put the galls with their leaves in a jar. Secure a small rag over the mouth of the jar with a rubber band. Keep the leaves damp and your jar outside in a place that's protected from rain. In early spring, the insects will come out. You will see tiny brown or black ant-like creatures, which may or may not have wings. The insects who emerge may not be the ones who made the galls. Other insects attack galls, kill the occupants, and take over their homes. When you're finished studying insects, let them go.

A Leaf Crown

Leaf crowns are easy and fun to make, by yourself or with your friends. And you can make them in the spring, summer, or autumn—depending on whether you want them to be green or brightly colored.

YOU'LL NEED:

12 large fresh leaves
Scissors
Pencil
Dandelions or other wildflowers (optional)

1 Try to collect large fresh leaves with long (at least 2- to 3-inch) stems. Don't use pressed leaves because they might crack. Although fresh leaves don't last long, they will make a beautiful crown.

2 Cut off each stem close to the base of the leaf and set it aside.

3 Overlap two leaves the long way, vein side up, as shown. Where the two leaves overlap, make two small holes about 1 inch apart with the tip of a pencil. The holes should be big enough for the stem to fit through.

4 To pin two leaves together, take a stem and push it up through one set of holes. Then bend the stem and push it down through the other set of holes.

5 Now "pin" a third leaf to one of the two leaves, following the directions in Steps 3 and 4. Keep adding leaves until your crown is big enough to fit your head. Then "pin" the first leaf to the last leaf to make a circle.

6 To decorate your crown with wildflowers, carefully tuck the stem of each flower underneath a leaf stem "pin."

7 If you make a crown with autumn leaves, you can gather bright leaves of many colors or you can use just yellow leaves—then it will look like gold!

Kitchen Collection

Y ou don't need fruit trees in your backyard to collect seeds. Look for seeds inside the fruits you bring home from the market.

Some seeds (such as apple seeds) have a thin covering; others (like the seeds of plums or peaches)  are inside a hard pit. With a hammer and an adult's help, a hard pit can be cracked open and the seed released. Also look for seeds inside apricots, avocados, cherries, grapefruits, grapes, lemons, oranges, papayas, pears, persimmons, and watermelons.

Magic With Cones

Ripe brown cones close up tight when it's wet out in order to protect their seeds. In dry weather, their winged seeds can fly far away on a breeze and find a good place to grow. But if the seeds came out when it was raining, they would become wet and heavy and fall straight to the ground.

Take an open brown cone, and sprinkle it with water. After about ten minutes you'll see it begin to close; in about an hour the scales will be shut. If you let it dry, the scales will open again in a few hours. Cones will open and shut whether they have seeds inside them or not.

This is an excellent magic trick to try on your friends: Secretly wet a cone before you show it to them, and then say you are "magically" going to make the cone close.

Leaf Art

Here are two different ways to make leaf paintings. Once they are dry, hang them on your wall, mount them in a scrapbook, or make notecards with them. Simply fold a piece of paper in half and do your painting on either side.

Autumn leaves are stiffer than green leaves and easier to handle for these projects.

Leaf Prints

Using leaves you can create a beautiful picture.

YOU'LL NEED:

Newspaper
Unpressed autumn leaves
Paint brush
Poster paint in various
    colors
Colored construction paper
    or white paper

1 Cover a work space with plenty of newspaper.

2 Choose several leaves with interesting shapes and vein patterns.

3 Use a brush or your fingers to paint the underside of each leaf (where the veins are) with poster paint.

4 Carefully pick up the wet leaf by the stem and place it, paint side down, on a piece of colored construction paper or white paper.

5 Cover the leaf with another piece of paper and rub gently but firmly. Carefully take up the top piece of paper, then lift the leaf by its stem.

6 Repeat with several more leaves if you want, using different paint colors. To overlap leaf patterns, allow the first leaf print to dry before doing the next one.

Leaf Silhouettes

This is a painting of just the outside edge of your leaf.

Leaf Art
by Kevin

YOU'LL NEED:

Newspaper
Unpressed leaf
Poster paint
Paintbrush, ½ to 1 inch wide
Construction paper or white
paper

1 Spread plenty of newspaper on your work surface.

2 Choose a leaf with lots of lobes or big teeth.

3 Place the leaf on a piece of paper, and hold it down with one hand. Paint all around the leaf, from the edge of the leaf onto the paper, using short outward strokes.

4 Carefully lift the leaf by its stem. Let the painting dry.

Autumn Collage

U se colorful leaves, pods, seeds, and cones to make an autumn collage. Not everything has to be whole—this project works well even with bits and pieces of things you've collected.

YOU'LL NEED:

Pencil
Cardboard or oaktag, any size
Page from coloring book (optional)
White paste
Pressed leaves, pods, seeds, cones, whole and pieces
Découpage glue (optional)

1 Make a drawing in pencil on your cardboard. It could be of a tree, butterfly, flower, or a scene of mountains and birds. Or cut out a picture from a coloring book and paste it onto your cardboard.

2 Spread some paste in one area and start arranging some of your tree collection. Work on one section at a time and try to get a good balance of leaves and seeds and whatever else you've collected. When you have finished, let your collage dry for two days.

3 If you'd like, paint your collage with découpage glue to give it a shiny finish.

Make a Bark Rubbing

Bark covers and protects the tree trunk. As a trunk grows wider, its bark stretches and cracks. The bark of each type of tree cracks in its own special way—some peels off, some splits, and some makes deep furrows.

Make a bark rubbing of your favorite tree.

YOU'LL NEED:

Masking tape
Piece of unlined paper
Crayon of any color

1 Tape a piece of paper to the trunk of a tree with an interesting bark pattern.

2 Remove the paper from the crayon. Rub the side of the crayon back and forth over the paper.

Soon you will begin to see the pattern of the bark on your paper.

Make bark rubbings of trees with different kinds of bark. Find a trunk with smooth bark and another with very rough bark.

Leaf Pals

If you don't live in a climate where leaves turn brilliant colors in autumn, why not exchange leaves through the mail with a friend or relative who does? Leaves that grow near you may be hard for your leaf pal to find, too.

Or speak to your teacher. It would be fun for your whole class to exchange leaves with children from a school in a different part of the country.

Always press leaves before sending them to someone else, and mail them between layers of thin cardboard for extra protection.